How to Use This Book

Each page of this booklet features a Writing Bug prompt and a "Bug in Your Ear" set of tips. Each page is numbered and you'll also find this box at the top right of each worksheet.

You can use this space to mark the Bugs you'd like to keep or to mark grades or place gold stars after students have completed work on the reproduced sheets.

Note: Education World grants classroom teachers the right to use these copyrighted materials for educational purposes.

Instant Writing-Prompt Worksheets!

Hold an 8½" x 11" sheet of blank, lined paper at the fold in this book.

Place the sheet and the book on the photocopier so that the Writing Bug you want becomes the top of the reproduced worksheet!

Make your copies!

A Flexible Classroom Resource

Writing Bugs can be used "on the fly," by substitute teachers, or, if you have time to preview the Bugs and plan for them, as part of your overall course of writing instruction.

Enjoy!

More Ways to "Bug" Your Student Writers!

Writing Bug Watch

Timed writing tests are increasingly a part of life, and the Writing Bug can help you prepare your students for those tests. Here's a three-part method you might find useful to implement over the period of a week or so:

1. First, do a Writing Bug prompt without timing and without a quantity goal.

2. Next, set a goal for a quantity of writing appropriate for your students — a paragraph with at least five sentences, for example. Instead of imposing a time limit, however, simply say, "Let's see how fast you can all accomplish this!"

3. Finally, more closely simulate the parameters of your state's timed writing tests by assigning, for example, a five-paragraph essay to be drafted in 45 minutes.

Writing Bug Club

Have students share their Writing Bug-inspired pieces, either by reading their work aloud, by posting them on a bulletin board, or by placing them in a "lending library." Have a mock awards ceremony where every kid wins a prize with a fun name, like "Most Bug-Like," "Best Tickler of the Thorax," or "The Antenna Award."

Cross-Editing

Have students work in pairs or in teams to suggest changes such as spelling or grammar adjustments to each other, gradually moving up to suggesting more significant revisions to strengthen a piece.

Publication

Use the Writing Bugs to encourage contributions to your school publications, or to inspire the creation of a new publication for student writing!

Table of Contents

Name: _____

It's Great to Be My Age

How old are you? Write your age on the lines in the headline below.

_____ Reasons Being _____ Years Old Is Great
(Your age)   *(Your age)*

Writing Bug

Bug in Your Ear

I don't mean to "bug" you, but you might...

- come up with as many reasons as possible why being the age you are today is great.
- narrow your list down to the best reasons for being your age. If you are six years old, you should narrow the list to six reasons; if you are ten years old, you should have ten reasons.
- check your writing for errors in spelling, grammar, and punctuation.

Name: _____

Alphabetical Story

Have some fun with this one! Try to write a story in which the first word of the story begins with the letter *A*, the second word begins with *B*, the third word begins with *C*, and so on.

I don't mean to "bug" you, but you might...
- *use a dictionary to help you write your story.*
- *try to create a story that makes sense.*
- *check your writing for errors in spelling, grammar and punctuation.*

Name: _____

If I Could Be Any Person in History

If I could be any famous person in history, I would be…

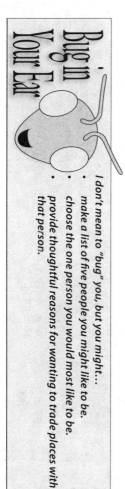

Bug in Your Ear

- I don't mean to "bug" you, but you might…
- make a list of five people you might like to be.
- choose the one person you would most like to be.
- provide thoughtful reasons for wanting to trade places with that person.

Name: _____

April Fool!

Think tall tale. Think big lie. Think up a tale so tall that it is impossible to believe. Then share the tale with a friend as if it is the honest truth. Just when you have your friend believing the tale *could* be true, end it with the words *April Fool!*

Bug in Your Ear

I don't mean to "bug" you, but you might…

• *write down some ideas that would be very difficult to believe.*

• *combine some of your best ideas into a very tall tale that is not true at all.*

• *be prepared to share your tale with your classmates— with a straight face!*

Name: _____

Writing Bug

Bad Manners

Imagine you live in a world where everybody has bad manners. Write a conversation between two people. At least one of those people should have *awful* manners!

Bug in Your Ear

I don't mean to "bug" you, but you might...

- *make a list of good manners. That will help you think about the things a person with bad manners might do.*
- *include in your story at least five examples of bad manners.*
- *use quotation marks in your story to show when somebody is talking.*

Name: _____

Best Friends

_____ is my best friend.

(Fill in the blank with the name of your best friend.)

_____ is my best friend because...

(He/She)

Bug in Your Ear

I don't mean to "bug" you, but you might...

- write a list of 20 qualities that a best friend might have.
- tell about the most important of those qualities in your writing.
- tell about the real events that will help others understand why this person is your best friend.

Name: _____

The Best Lesson

The best lesson I ever learned was...

_____

_____

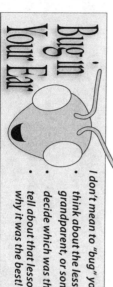

Bug in Your Ear

I don't mean to "bug" you, but you might...

- *think about the lessons you have learned from a parent, a grandparent, or someone else.*
- *decide which was the most valuable lesson you learned.*
- *tell about that lesson—be sure to give thoughtful reasons why it was the best!*

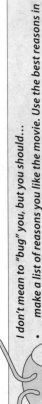

Name: _____

The Best Movie Ever

My favorite movie of all time is...

Bug in Your Ear

I don't mean to "bug" you, but you should...

- *make a list of reasons you like the movie. Use the best reasons in your writing.*
- *give at least three reasons you think it is the best movie.*
- *end your writing by summarizing your thoughts.*

Name: _____

Writing Bug

The Best Pet

Forget about cats and dogs. Don't even think about fish or gerbils. I think the best animal to have as a pet is...

Bug in Your Ear!

I don't mean to "bug" you, but you might...

- *think about an unusual animal that would make an interesting pet.*
- *make a list of reasons you would like that pet. Use your best reasons in your story.*
- *use words that will help convince others that your pet is the best pet.*

Name: _____

A Book Is Like a Garden

Read the following Chinese proverb:
"A book is like a garden carried in a pocket."

What does the proverb mean to you? Explain the meaning in your own words.

Bug in Your Ear

I don't mean to "bug" you, but...

- think for a few minutes about the proverb's meaning.
- make your writing stronger by telling about an example in your life that relates to the proverb.
- check your writing for errors in spelling, grammar, and punctuation.

Name: _____

Cheer Up!

Author Mark Twain once said, "The best way to cheer yourself up is to try to cheer somebody else up." What does that quote say to you?

I don't mean to "bug" you, but...

- *think for a few minutes about the quote's meaning.*
- *make your writing stronger by telling about an example in your life that relates to the quote.*
- *check your writing for errors in spelling, grammar, and punctuation.*

Cross-Country Trip

You are about to drive across the country.
You can take one person with you. Whom
would you choose?

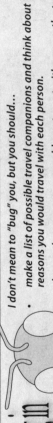

Bug in Your Ear

I don't mean to "bug" you, but you should...

- *make a list of possible travel companions and think about reasons you would travel with each person.*
- *choose the person you would most want with you on the trip.*
- *be sure to include strong and thoughtful reasons in your writing.*

Name: _____

Writing Bug

A Different Kind of Day

I knew today was going to be different when my mother woke me up and said...

_____

Bug in Your Ear

I don't mean to "bug" you, but you might...

- make a list of strange things that might happen on a day that is very different from most days. Use the most unusual things in your story.

- use quotation marks when somebody is talking.

- check your writing for errors of spelling, grammar, and punctuation.

Name: _____

First Day of School

Today is the second day of school. Now that the first day of the new school year is behind you, write a summary of the things you did on the first day of school.

Bug in Your Ear

I don't mean to "bug" you, but you might…

- make a list of ten things you did on the first day of school. Start your list with what you did first thing in the morning and end it at the end of the day.

- write a summary that includes at least five things you did during the first day of school.

- check your writing for errors of spelling, grammar, and punctuation.

Name: _____

Writing Bug

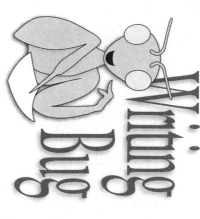

Not Your Average Grandmother

My friend's grandmother is different. When she came to visit last month, she had dyed her hair purple. But now she has topped that! When she showed up yesterday, she...

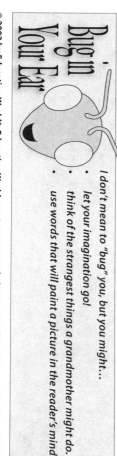

Bug in Your Ear

- *I don't mean to "bug" you, but you might...*
- *let your imagination go!*
- *think of the strangest things a grandmother might do.*
- *use words that will paint a picture in the reader's mind.*

Name: _____

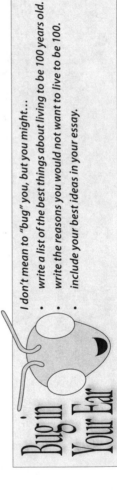

Happy 100th Birthday!

Would you want to live to be 100 years old?

I don't mean to "bug" you, but you might...

- *write a list of the best things about living to be 100 years old.*
- *write the reasons you would not want to live to be 100.*
- *include your best ideas in your essay.*

Name: _____

Writing Bug

Super Hero

You are starring as the super hero in a new movie. What special powers do you have? How do you use those powers to do heroic things?

Bug in Your Ear

I don't mean to "bug" you, but you might...

- think about some of the powers other super heroes have.
- choose the super powers you would like to have. Maybe you can come up with special powers no other super hero has!
- describe in your story how you use those powers to do good things.

Name: _____

If I Were the Teacher

If I were the teacher, I would...

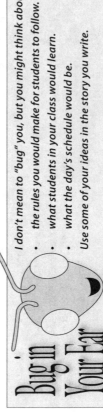

Bug in Your Ear

I don't mean to "bug" you, but you might think about...

• the rules you would make for students to follow.
• what students in your class would learn.
• what the day's schedule would be.

Use some of your ideas in the story you write.

Name: _____

Inquiring Minds Want to Know

Following are the headlines of four stories that were published in tabloid newspapers. Write the news story that might have gone with one of these headlines.

"Girl with 14 Fingers Wins Typing Contest"

"Man Eats Books!"

"Dog Lands Plane after Pilot Has Heart Attack"

"Man Wins $25,000 Bet by Swallowing Watermelon Whole"

I don't mean to "bug" you, but you should include...

- *who, what, when, where, why, and how.*
- *made-up quotes from people involved in the story.*
- *a picture to go with the news story.*

19

Name: _____

The Greatest Invention Ever

I think the greatest invention ever is the...

Bug in Your Ear!

I don't mean to "bug" you, but you might...

• *make a list of ten inventions you think have been among the most important.*

• *choose the invention you think is the most important one ever.*

• *include at least three reasons you think that invention is the most important.*

Writing Bug

Name: _____

Writing Bug

A Noise in the Kitchen

When I walked into the kitchen, I heard something move in the cupboard. I....

Bug in Your Ear

I don't mean to "bug" you, but it might help to...

- *think about what went through your mind when you heard the noise.*
- *make a list of adjectives that describe how you felt.*
- *come up with a surprise ending!*

Writing Bug

Name: _____

Lost in the Middle of Nowhere

Our old car rattled to a dead stop in the middle of nowhere. We sat for a moment to think about what we should do next. Then…

Bug in Your Ear

I don't mean to "bug" you, but you might…

· think about what it might be like to be totally lost. How would you feel?

· use good adjectives to describe the place in which you are lost.

· think about three ways in which you might solve your problem. Use the best way in your story.

Name: _____

I Need Your Advice

Think of a famous person you admire. You would like to write to that person to ask his or her advice—and now is your chance. Write your letter below.

I don't mean to "bug" you, but you should...

- *think of three famous people you might like to write to for advice.*
- *choose the one person you would most like to write to. Use the correct friendly letter format.*
- *tell the person why you think she or he is special and why you have chosen to write to her or him.*

Name: _____

No More Smiling!

The city council in your city just passed a new law. From now on, smiling is against the law. You wonder…

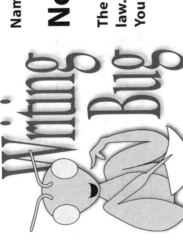

Bug in Your Ear

I don't mean to "bug" you, but you might think about these questions:

- Why did lawmakers pass this law?
- What would your city be like if nobody smiled?
- What might happen to people who break the law?

Name: _____

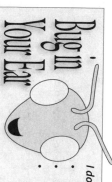

Open at Your Own Risk!

When I arrived at school today, there was a big orange sign on my desk. The black lettering on the sign said, "Open at Your Own Risk!" I...

Bug in Your Ear

- I don't mean to "bug" you, but...
- let your imagination go!
- use words that help the reader sense your fear.
- try to build some suspense into your story.

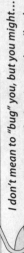

Name: _____

Postcard from Another Planet

You are the first human to land on another planet.
Describe what you see and how you feel.

Bug in Your Ear

I don't mean to "bug" you, but you might...

- *make a list of adjectives to describe the scene you see.*
- *make a list of adjectives to describe your feelings about being the first human to explore the planet.*
- *include the best adjectives as you write an excellent description.*

Name: _____

Writing Bug

Rich or Smart?

If you had a chance to be the richest person in the world or the smartest person in the world, which would you choose?

Bug in Your Ear

I don't mean to "bug" you, but you might...

- make two columns on a sheet of paper. Label one Richest and the other Smartest.
- think about the benefits of being richest and smartest, and write your ideas under those headings.
- use your ideas to help you write a thoughtful paragraph.

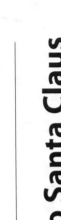

Name: _____

A Letter to Santa Claus

Dear Santa,

Today I am not writing about myself. I am writing about somebody else. I would like to ask you to...

I don't mean to "bug" you, but you should be sure to...

- *use the correct form for a friendly letter.*
- *write a thoughtful letter.*
- *give good reasons for your request.*

Bug in Your Ear

Name: _____

Building a Snowperson

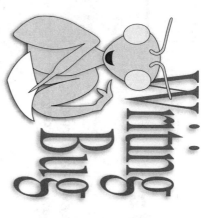

How do you make a snowman or a snowwoman? A child who lives near the equator might have no idea, so your job is to write detailed directions for building a snowperson.

I don't mean to "bug" you, but you should…

- *picture in your mind the steps to make a snowperson. Make a list of the steps.*
- *be sure your words paint a picture for the person reading them.*
- *don't leave out any steps!*

Bug in Your Ear

Name: _____

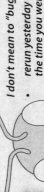

Yesterday Was a Special Day

Every day is a special day. Why was yesterday so special? Write five good reasons yesterday was a special day.

Bug in Your Ear

I don't mean to "bug" you, but you might...

- rerun yesterday in your mind—from the time you woke up until the time you went to bed. Make notes about what happened.
- choose five things that made it a very special day.
- check your writing for errors in spelling, grammar, and punctuation.

Name: _____

When Spider Webs Unite

An old Ethiopian proverb says, "When spider webs unite, they can tie up a lion." What does that proverb mean to you?

Bug in Your Ear

I don't mean to "bug" you, but…

- think for a few minutes about the proverb's meaning.
- make your writing stronger by telling about an example in your life that relates to the proverb.
- check your writing for errors in spelling, grammar, and punctuation.

Name: _____

Springtime Storm

It's springtime—and time for spring storms. Think about taking a walk in a spring storm. Use all your senses to describe the storm.

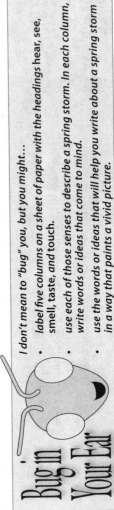

Bug in Your Ear

I don't mean to "bug" you, but you might…

- label five columns on a sheet of paper with the headings *hear, see, smell, taste,* and *touch.*

- use each of those senses to describe a spring storm. In each column, write words or ideas that come to mind.

- use the words or ideas that will help you write about a spring storm in a way that paints a vivid picture.

Name: _____

My Personal Tongue Twister

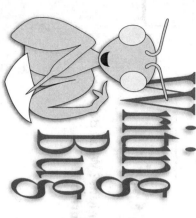

Did you know that Peter Piper picked a peck of pickled peppers? Did you know that Ruby Rugby's brother bought and brought her back some rubber baby buggy bumpers? Peter and Ruby are the subjects of two well-known tongue twisters. Now is your chance to make up your own tongue twister, using your name as the subject.

I don't mean to "bug" you, but you might...

- *write a list of 50 words that begin with the same letter as your first name. Be sure to include nouns, verbs, and adjectives.*

- *see whether you can put at least six of those words together to make a tongue twister.*

- *try your tongue twister on your classmates.*

33

Name: _____

Tune In or Turn Off

Is watching TV a good thing for kids? What do you think? Should kids tune in or turn off?

Bug in Your Ear

I don't mean to "bug" you, but you might...

- make a list of good things about TV and another list of bad things about TV.
- decide which list offers better ideas.
- take a strong stand one way or the other—don't be wishy-washy!

Name: _____

Turkey Terror

It was the week before Thanksgiving. You could tell the turkeys were nervous because...

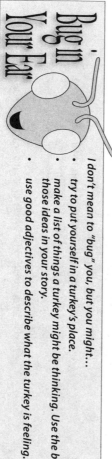

Bug in Your Ear

I don't mean to "bug" you, but you might...

- try to put yourself in a turkey's place.
- make a list of things a turkey might be thinking. Use the best of those ideas in your story.
- use good adjectives to describe what the turkey is feeling.

Name: _____

Who, When, Where

Choose one item from each category.
Then write a story based on your choices.

WHO	WHERE	WHEN
a clown	Antarctica	in the middle of the night
a police office	in an underground cave	during pre-historic times
a mathematician	aboard a hot-air balloon	in the 1970s
a dentist	Jupiter	on the first day of school

I don't mean to "bug" you, but you should...

- *make connections between the who, where, and when that make sense or might really have happened.*
- *show you understand something about the person, the place and the time.*
- *check your writing for errors of spelling, grammar, and punctuation.*

36

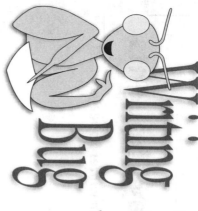

Name: _____

Describing Winifred Witch

Winifred Witch was a sight to see! She...

Bug in Your Ear

I don't mean to "bug" you, but you might...

- picture Winifred in your mind before you write.
- write a list of 20 adjectives to describe her hair, clothing, and other features. Use some of those adjectives as you write your description.
- draw a picture of Winifred Witch to go with your writing.

Name: _____

Winter Holiday Thoughts

My favorite thing about the winter holidays is...

Bug in Your Ear

I don't mean to "bug" you, but you might think about...
- what makes the winter holidays special.
- what the holidays mean to you.
- your favorite memories of holidays past.

Name: _____

I Wish I Had a Million

Complete the following sentence with any word except "dollars" or other money word.

I wish I had a million _____ because...

I wish I had a million _____

Bug in Your Ear

I don't mean to "bug" you, but you might...

- make a list of five words that could complete the sentence.
- choose the best word.
- provide at least three reasons you would not want to have a million _____.

Name: _____

The Worst Invention Ever

I think the worst invention ever is the...

I don't mean to "bug" you, but you might...
- make a list of ten inventions you think the world could do without.
- choose the invention you think is the worst one ever.
- include at least three reasons you think that invention is the worst.

Name: _____

Writing Bug

An Interview With a President

If you could interview any U.S. president, which one would you choose? Why? What questions would you ask that president?

Bug in Your Ear

I don't mean to "bug" you, but you might...

- *think about three presidents you might like to interview. Choose the one you would like to interview the most.*
- *give three reasons to explain your choice.*
- *write at least three thoughtful questions you would ask that president.*

41

Name: _____

Genie in a Bottle

You're cleaning out the basement. You find a strange-looking bottle behind a box. When you dust off the bottle, a genie appears! Then...

Bug in Your Ear

I don't mean to "bug" you, but you might...

- let your imagination go!
- use words that help the reader sense your surprise.
- try to build some excitement into your story.

Name: _____

My Proudest Moment

My proudest moment was the time I...

I don't mean to "bug" you, but you might...

- *think about three times you felt proud about something you did.*
- *choose the time that you were the most proud of an achievement.*
- *tell details about that accomplishment and how you achieved it.*

Name: _____

What Would You Do?

You're in the park on a Saturday afternoon. You see a classmate being bullied by two other students from your school. What would you do?

If you run out of room, use the back of this page or another sheet of paper.

Bug in Your Ear

I don't mean to "bug" you, but you might...

- write down three actions you could take.
- write about the action you think would be the best one.
- check your writing for errors of spelling, grammar, and punctuation.